Tavern Signs

Contemporary Hooked Rugs and the Stories They Tell

Karl and Mary Jo Gimber

Dear Jen, Dave, Kate, and Lulu
        Thought you might like to see what we
have been working on since last October (the self-
publishing part). Found 26 corrections in this one and
change them in the next proof - Happy Easter. Mom + Dad. Grandpa
                                                                        and Grandma
                                                                            xoxo

Publisher: Goat & Palette, PO Box 16, Carversville, Pa 18913

Photographer: Lee Rutherford, www.rutherfordcamera.com

ISBN: 13:978-14752277932

ISBN: 10:147-5227930

Title Page Photo: Swan with Two Necks Tavern

The tavern named the Swan with Two Nicks evolved into the Swan with Two Necks. This type of corruption frequently occurred with tavern names. In early America farmers marked and registered their animals as a means of identification. Cattle were branded; hogs and sheep had distinct cuts in their ears and, in England domestic birds such as swans, ducks and geese had their beaks nicked in a similar manner. The rug was designed by Mary Jo and hooked by Karl with recycled wool in 2012. Size: 38 ½" x 32 ½".[89]

Dedicated to our first teacher, Edie

Acknowledgments

We want to express our deepest gratitude to those who have encouraged, taught, and helped us in our rug hooking adventure and especially to the Hunterdon County Rug Artisans Guild members for their friendship and inspiration.

Contents

Introduction

We have had a lifelong interest in 18th and 19th century American history and the decorative arts. In 2002 we purchased a hooked mat at a local auction. The woman who hooked it was in the audience and introduced herself. We learned that she was conducting a rug hooking workshop for beginners at the Mercer Museum in Doylestown, Pennsylvania. We attended and as the saying goes, "We were hooked."

Since that time we have been working on a series of hooked rugs based on antique tavern, trade and farm signs. More than 100 rugs have been completed so far. Many of the rugs are based on old signs found in folk art books, auction catalogs and history books. We are attracted to signs with a unique design, or a tavern with an interesting story or name. Many times we find only the name of the tavern. Older books do not contain the graphics that we expect today but they remain an excellent source of tavern names and their histories.

We work primarily with wool from recycled clothing found at local thrift stores, rummage sales, flea markets, and from friends. After cleaning the wool, it can be used *as is* or overdyed. We save labels from garments and sewn them on the back of the rug. Some are from haberdashers and department stores no longer in business and historic in their own right. When using recycled garments, we feel a connection with the early rug hookers who went to their rag bags and pulled out whatever fabric they found to use for their rugs.

Each year we may attend a rug hooking workshop or two. However, much of what we have learned has come from hooking our rugs and from members of our local Hunterdon County Rug Artisans Guild (www.hcrag.com).

The purpose of this book is to share our interest in early American history and traditional rug hooking by telling the stories behind our tavern sign rugs. Mary Jo often incorporates a peeking face as her signature on rugs she has designed. Look for them!

Taverns in Early America

Today people are accustomed to finding several motels at the exits of most major highways. That was not the case in early America. Old Indian trails served as links between the small towns that were forming in the thirteen colonies. Travel was slow and arduous and there was no place to stay to get out of the elements other than private homes that might be found along the way.

Travelers approached private homes requesting lodging which placed unwanted demands on citizens such as William Hartley of Chester County, Pennsylvania who finally petitioned for a tavern license in 1740 because his house was "continually infested with travelers who call for and demand necessaries, and that he has been at great charges in supplying them with bedding and their horses with proper provender without any payment." [1]

As the trails became roads, taverns started to appear at intersections and at river crossings. Eventually taverns would be found 10 to 20 miles apart which was the average distance that could be travelled by horseback in a day.

Travelers had increasing difficulty identifying the tavern from other buildings. In 1672 Connecticut enacted an ordinance that states:

> "Every person licensed for common entertainment shall have some suitable sign set up in view of all passengers for the direction of strangers where to go where they may have entertainment." [2]

New England laws governing the creation of new towns often required that one home in each town be declared a tavern for accommodating travelers. [3]

Only upstanding citizens could operate taverns and laws placed restrictions on hours, prices and how much alcohol could be served to customers. Hingham, Massachusetts issued a license in 1702 giving permission to a tavernkeeper to:

> "sell Strong Waters provided he sent his customers home at reasonable hours, with ability to keep their legs."[4]

Taverns were patronized by travelers and members of the local community. Activities in the better city taverns centered on economic life, every day business transactions and events such as auctions, trials and elections.[5] Newspapers could be found at the tavern and provided the basis for lively discussions on issues of the time. By 1763 there were only 48 post offices in operation, so taverns served as the repository for mail and packages in towns without a post office.[6]

A close association existed between early taverns and churches. Church services during the 17th and 18th centuries were all day affairs held in unheated meetinghouses. Taverns with roaring fires and spirits provided an opportunity to thaw out between the morning and afternoon sermons.[13] An application to establish a tavern often required that the tavern be located within close proximity to the meetinghouse. A Boston ordinary keeper in 1651 was granted permission to keep a tavern "provided hee keepe it neare the new meeting-house."[7] If the meetinghouse had not yet been built, services were often held in the local tavern.

Origins of Signboards

Little is known about the use of signboards in the ancient world, although Greek writers do make reference to them. Merchants selling their products in the open bazaars of Egypt did not need signboards. Their goods exposed for sale were sufficient to attract attention.[8] The use of signs appears to have started with the Romans; signs made of stone or terra-cotta were discovered in ancient ruins. One of the earliest signs came from the Roman practice of hanging a bush of evergreens on a building to indicate the sale of wine.[9] During the Middle Ages houses of the nobility were used as hostelries when the families were away. Their coats of arms decorated with images of lions, dragons, deer and various types of flora and fauna which could be found on their castles, armor, and needle work would later be used on tavern signboards.[10]

Early Forms of Advertising

Signboards made it easier for an illiterate population to identify a tavern or shop. Street signs and house numbers were generally non-existent. Reference to a tavern sign was frequently used when giving direction such as "go to the Sign of the Boar."

Many early tavern signs relied on images without text to attract patrons. Images of a punch bowl or a bottle with wine glasses identified the services or products available. Text was added to signs, images became bolder and more elaborate, and the size of signs increased, and many were three dimensional. Large signs hung further out over the road creating safety hazards and ordinances were enacted to control the size and location of signs.

Early signboards usually had single images. Signs with multiple images such as the Crown & Mitre, Hen & Chicks, and Light House & Anchor came later and were easily understood by the public. However the Unicorn & Pearl, Bull & Bedpost, and Three Nuns & Hare were puzzling.[11] Quaint combinations resulted in the following item which appeared in *British Apollo* in 1710:

"I'm amazed at the signs
As I pass through the town,
To see the odd mixture;
A Magpie and Crown,
The Whale and the Crow,

The Razor and Hen,
The Leg and Seven Stars,
The Axe and the Bottle,
The Tun and the Lute,
The Eagle and the Child,
The Shovel and Boot."[11]

In *The History of Signboards from the Earliest Times to the Present Day*, renowned historians, Larwood and Hotten, offered several possible explanations for this phenomenon:

- Shopkeepers and tavern owners moved to another location and combined the old sign with the sign at the new location, especially if the new location was a recognized landmark.
- A journeyman starting his business added the image of the master with whom he apprenticed to his own sign.
- Words became corrupted over time.
- Whimsical images and combinations were used to attract patrons.

Evolution of Terms

The terms tavern and inn are often used interchangeably today. In colonial times, these terms had different meanings. "Ordinary" was one of the first words used to describe a public house where patrons ate whatever was being served. An "ordinary" normally limited itself to serving cider, ale and rum.[12] The term "ordinary" was replaced in the colonies by the end of the 17th century. Courts in New Jersey began to use the word "tavern" as early as 1700. In New England and New York, the term "tavern" was usually used, while in Pennsylvania "inn" was more common.

The terms "inn" and "tavern" were used interchangeably. Patrons could get meals at any time and were offered a choice food and drink. The difference between the terms was blurred by the time of the American Revolution.

During the revolution, France supported the colonies in the struggle against the British. French influence was soon seen in ways other than military and financial. Constance Green in the *History of Naugatuck* wrote:

"Out of deference to American enthusiasm for things French in this period before the War of 1812, when Lafayette's memory was still fresh and any enemy of Great Britain was a friend of America, the proprietor, Ahira Collins, set up his sign to read 'Collins Hotel,' using the French word 'hotel' instead of the older English label, tavern or inn."[14]

Consequently, the first use of the term "hotel" appeared in a 1779 advertisement for Ephraim

Minor's Hotel in New London, Connecticut.[15] Text such as "entertainment" or "entertainment for man and horse" appears in many instances on old tavern signs. "Entertainment" had a far different meaning in the 18th and 19th centuries indicating to the weary traveler that food, drink and lodging were available for him and his horse.

Coffee was first introduced to the British in London during the 1650s and it appeared in Boston in 1678. Although tea was the major non-alcoholic beverage of the time, it was enjoyed primarily in the home. Coffee gained in popularity during the 18th century and was served in taverns referred to as coffee houses.[16] Coffee houses attracted merchants and were places where commerce was transacted.

Where to Find Tavern and Trade Signs

Historical information on early British and American tavern and trade signs can be found in many places:

- Books on the history of tavern and trade signs
- Signs in the collections of the Shelburne Museum, Historic Deerfield, Old Sturbridge Village, the Connecticut Historical Society, Bucks County Historical Society, the Abby Aldrich Rockefeller Folk Art Museum, and the Pocumtuck Valley Memorial Hall Museum
- Museum and historical society publications
- Antique shows and antique shops
- Auctions and auction catalogues
- The internet and online vendors
- Antique trade publications - *Maine Antique Digest, Art and Antiques Weekly*

(See *bibliography* for more information.)

The Flagon & Trencher Society

The Flagon and Trencher Society is a lineage society dedicated to celebrating tavern keeping ancestors who operated taverns on or before July 4, 1776. We learned of the Society from an article in *Early American Life Magazine* entitled *Celebrating Tavern-Keeping Ancestors* in the August 2009 issue and joked about the possibility of finding a tavernkeeper ancestor. We discovered from The Flagon & Trencher website (www.flagonandtrencher.org) that the Society had published thirteen volumes of tavernkeeper biographies for qualifying ancestors of Flagon and Trencher members and we ordered the set for our research. After receiving the volumes, we found three of Mary Jo's tavern keeping ancestors who had previously been documented by qualifying members. Mary Jo was able to become a member of the Society with little additional research.

William Clough Bloss

William Clough Bloss is one of Mary Jo's favorite tavern keeping cousins. He owned a tavern on the Erie Canal in Brighton, New York and during the Spiritual Awakening that swept New York in the 19th century Bloss became an early advocate of the temperance movement. In 1826 he poured the entire liquid contents of his tavern into the Erie Canal! After moving his family to Rochester, Bloss joined the anti-slavery movement, helped organize a local anti-slavery society with African American minister, Thomas James, and signed a call for the first anti-slavery convention in Utica, New York. When local papers refused to publish the society's by-laws and constitution, Bloss and other supporters started their own newspaper, *The Rights of Man.* The Bloss family home served as a stop on the *Underground Railroad* providing shelter for former slaves moving north. While serving in the legislature, Bloss attempted to change the state constitution in order to provide voting rights for African Americans and proposed the Free School Law allowing equal rights of education without segregation to all persons regardless of color. A supporter of women's rights, Bloss endorsed women's suffrage as early as 1838.[90]

Exercise Conant Tavern

Exercise Conant, one of Mary Jo's tavernkeeper ancestors, was the son of Governor Roger Conant, the founder of Salem, Massachusetts. In 1701, while living in Boston, Exercise Conant was granted a "license to Sell all Sorts drinck out of doors by Retaile." [17]

This rug was designed by Mary Jo based on the name and location of the tavern and hooked by Karl in 2012. Recycled wool was used *as is* for all but the corners, which were hooked with overdyed wool. Mary Jo's signature face appears on lower left side of inner oval. Size: 30"x38".

Domestic Animal Themes

Taverns named after animals were common in colonial America and England. Domestic animals such as bulls, cocks, boars, horses, and sheep were especially popular names for taverns and inns. Citizens could easily relate to the images making them more likely to be remembered. Animals on tavern signs came in an endless variety of colors such as the Red Cock, Golden Fleece and Blue Boar. Horses are among the most common images used on tavern signboards. However, it was uncommon for a tavern to be known simply as "The Horse Tavern." Most often colors were associated with the name such as the Black Horse, White Horse, Sorrel Horse, and occasionally the Red Horse. Two of the most popular early American taverns - the White Horse and the Black Horse - have English origins.

Exotic Animal Themes

Animals found on the earliest signs were often inspired by English heraldry. These signs featured boars, dragons, eagles, lions, and unicorns with lions being the most popular. Our colonial ancestors were fascinated with exotic animals from foreign lands. Camels, crocodiles, elephants, and tigers all appear on tavern signs. Prior to the advent of the circus in the 1830s, showmen with one or two exotic animals would travel from town to town exhibiting their creatures at the local tavern for a small fee. In exchange for the additional business generated by curious neighbors who came to see the animal shows, tavernkeepers would normally provide housing in the barn. On March 21, 1796 the *Connecticut Courant* advertised the following spectacle: "To the curious, a beautiful African Lion, to be seen every day in the week, Sundays excepted, at Mr. Joseph Pratt's Tavern in Hartford."[18]

The White Horse Tavern (Ipswich)

Robert Andrews and his son, John, are two of Mary Jo's tavern keeping ancestors. Both kept the White Horse Tavern in Ipswich, Massachusetts. "Corporal" John Andrews, as he was known, lost his license in 1658. Some accounts say that this resulted from charges being brought against him for his failure to observe the law with regard to the sale of spirits. Another account indicates that his license was revoked after he pulled down the signboard of a rival tavernkeeper. A petition by Ipswich townsmen led to his tavern license being revoked.[19]

We had an opportunity to visit Ipswich and saw the old tavern building which is now a private residence. The original signboard no longer exists. Mary Jo designed the rug in remembrance of her tavernkeeper ancestors. Karl hooked the rug in 2012. Recycled wool was used *as is* for most of the rug. Some wool was overdyed. New wool was used for the green background and corners. Size: 29"x38".

G. D. Witt Crocodile Tavern

The G. D. Witt family members from Kingston, New York were patriots who owned a grist mill and the Crocodile Tavern. The family provided flour for General George Washington's starving army at Valley Forge during the harsh winter of 1777. The Crocodile Tavern was a popular meeting place for Ulster County's Revolutionary War leaders. On November 16, 1782 George Washington stopped on his way from West Point to thank those who supplied flour five years earlier. In G. D. Witt's home country of Holland, a stuffed crocodile was the traditional symbol for an apothecary, which often doubled as a secret drinking establishment. The crocodile has come down through history associated with drinking and taverns.[20]

Mary Jo adapted the pattern from an image of the original sign found in an auction catalog. Karl hooked it in 2008. Three different dye formulas were used on white and off-white skirts to produce the wool for the sky. A dark pleated skirt provided the *as is* wool for the contrast needed behind the tavern name. Size: 24 "x 44".

The Unicorn Tavern

The unicorn was a popular image found on tavern and trade signs in colonial America and England. It also represented the apothecary because the horn was believed to be an antidote for all poisons. Button makers, cutlers, razor makers, silk dyers, goldsmiths, and silversmiths also used the unicorn on their signboards. The unicorn represents purity and has religious and social meaning for Pennsylvania Germans. Unicorns are found in their fraktur drawings, redware, needlework, and paint decorated furniture.

Mary Jo designed the rug based on several sources – fraktur books, carousel figures and antique painted furniture. It was hooked by Karl in 2006. All recycled *as is* wool was used with the exception of the new green plaid in the border background. Camel colored sport coats and skirts were used for the central background. A variety of purple strips left over from other projects was used for the lettering. Size: 50" x 35".

The Elephant Hotel

During Roman times the elephant was a favorite symbol on tavern signs. In the Middle Ages, the elephant was nearly always represented with a castle on its back. [21]

The original sign, the basis for our rug design, is in the Bucks County Historical Society collection. The Elephant Hotel was established in Bedminster, Pennsylvania in 1848 and has two elements we often look for -- it is local and has a special story. There is a ghost story associated with the Elephant Hotel. In 1855 one hundred people tragically died in a train crash in the nearby community of Perkasie. A wagon driver carrying caskets stopped for a drink at the Elephant Hotel, but his wagon turned over as he arrived at the tavern. After the scattered bodies were returned to the caskets, one of the bodies was missing and the story of the ghost at the Elephant Hotel began. [22] In a more recent story, we learned from a friend who stopped at the Elephant with her husband in the 1970s that the tavernkeepers had a pet deer that walked around the tavern much like a pet cat or dog. Mary Jo adapted the pattern from the original sign. The rug was hooked by Karl in 2008. Size: 21" x 25".

Camel Inn (Hard Times)

Taverns were often located at ferry crossings to provide food, drink and lodging for travelers. There have been ferry crossings along the Delaware River since the early 1700s including one in a town known as Lumberton, Pennsylvania along River Road in Bucks County. The taverns associated with the crossing were for many years simply known by the name of the ferry owners. In the early 1800s the local economy was in recession and times were hard. The tavernkeeper took a discarded window shutter and with tar painted the words "Hard Times." It served as the tavern sign and soon the surrounding community was also known as Hard Times.

The 1830s economy rebounded with the building of the Delaware Canal. The tavern name changed to "The Sign of The Camel" for reasons that have been lost.[23] This is a curious name for a tavern since camels are known to travel great distances without drinking. In the early 1900s, The Cuttalossa Inn, which was named after the creek which flows nearby, was established in the miller's house across the road from the original tavern building. The Cuttalossa Inn became a popular destination for travelers visiting Bucks County. The inn is currently undergoing restoration. Mary Jo designed the rug to reflect the evolution of the name of the tavern. Karl hooked the rug in 2013. Material used includes new gray and white-check wool for the camel, dip dyed wool for the lettering and recycled skirts for the background. Size: 27 ½" x 22 ½".

Amphibian & Reptile Themes

It is rare to find taverns named after insects, amphibians or reptiles; however, there are some instances of frogs appearing on tavern signboards in England. Existing English records document the Three Frogs, Froghall and the Golden Frog taverns in old England.

Frog Pond Tavern

We are attracted to taverns and signboards with interesting names or stories which lend themselves to colorful hooked rugs such as the Frog Pond Tavern in Williamsburg, Virginia.

A Williamsburg Scrap Book, compiled by the Williamsburg Garden Club and published in 1950, describes a thriving tavern built in front of Williamsburg's biggest mud hole. The mud hole was located on the old stage road to Richmond at the western end of town. Every effort to drain or fill it was unsuccessful. It was a sizable pond which produced enough frogs to keep the tavern guests satisfied throughout the year. Eventually, it was known by these delicacies as the Frog Pond tavern. The tavernkeeper was Old by Jucks, a genial fellow known throughout the town.

The rug pattern was designed by Mary Jo and hooked by Karl in 2011. Overdyed recycled wool was used. Size: 27 ¼" x 20".

Nautical Themes

Taverns with nautical related names were popular with ship crews and those working on the wharfs in seaport communities up and down the Atlantic coast. These taverns served as sites for recruiting crews for upcoming voyages. Brightly painted images of The Ship, Captain's Cabin, Yankee Clipper, The Mermaid, and The Blue Anchor helped sailors and other patrons identify their favorite taverns. The "Inn for Sea Faring Men" operated in Annapolis in 1740, clearly attempted to appeal to mariners.

Blue Anchor Tavern

Anchor Inns were found in every early American seaport from Newport to Charlestown. In Philadelphia, the Blue Anchor Inn was built in 1682 making it the first in the city. It was under construction when William Penn first came to Philadelphia. Today, the complex appropriately known as Penn's Landing is built on the site of the Blue Anchor. The Blue Anchor on Havers Dock in Boston offered "Refreshment & Entertainment of Boatman & others coming from the Country and distance by Water."[25]

The rug pattern was adapted from the sign for the R. Hammon Inn in the Connecticut Historical Society collection and was hooked by Karl in 2005. Size: 23 ½" x33".

Mermaid Tavern

The Sign of the Mermaid was used by both tavern and shop keepers in England and America. Perhaps the most celebrated Mermaid Tavern was established in London as early as the late 1400s. In 1603 Sir Walter Raleigh established a literary club at The Mermaid with William Shakespeare and Ben Johnson among its members.[26]

Mermaids were also popular images etched into whale's teeth and other scrimshaw objects by sailors during long whaling voyages. The mermaid is frequently found on 18th century powder horns. When Karl was at Muhlenberg College in the early 1960s, he belonged to the Mermaid Tavern Society which met at the Allentown Art Museum each month. His art history professor would give a short lecture while members enjoyed a mug of ale.

Mary Jo used the Society's emblem in the design of the rug, which is based on an illustration in

Old English Cuts & Illustrations for Artists & Craftspeople. Karl hooked the rug in 2013 andused more new wool than usual in this rug. A striped wool scarf was used for the water and a light strip for the foam in the waves to create motion. Three textured green wools were used for the mermaid's tail and paisley in the waistband added a spark of color. Four shades of new textured golds and yellows were used for the hair. Size: 30 ½" x 38".

Sign of the Whale and Raven Tavern

Whaling was a major commercial activity in the early 19th century. The Sign of the Whale would have been found in coastal communities attracting seafaring patrons.

The pattern was designed and hooked by Karl in 2013. Recycled blue, green, aqua, and turquoise plaid skirts were used for the water. The whale was hooked with wool from gray textured sport coats. Several shades of gold and dark yellow were used for the background. Size: 36 ½" x 50".

Bird Themes

There are numerous American and English taverns named after fowl. Images of hens, cocks, pigeons, hawks, pheasants, and crows are just a few birds that flew in front of local taverns and shops. These images were relatable and appealing to the common man and in some cases had religious meanings that could be equally appealing. Bird signs came in a full rainbow of colors such as the Blue Cock, Golden Pheasant, Green Parrot, and Red Hen.

The Peacock Inn

Centuries ago the ancients believed that the flesh of the peacock would not decay.[27] Over time, religions adopted the peacock as a symbol of resurrection, eternal life and purity. Tavernkeepers, shopkeepers, silversmiths, hosiers, booksellers, lace men, silk dyers, and linen drapers used the image to project the quality of their services and products.[28]

In the 19th century, the voice of the peacock was often heard on Pennsylvania German farms. The peacock, a Christian symbol for immortality, appears in many Pennsylvania German decorative arts. It is found on china, fraktur drawings, redware plates, tin trays, mirrors, quilts, and samplers.

Ideas for rug patterns can be found in many places. Auction catalogues are a favorite source of inspiration. We found the image of the peacock on what was described as a mid-19th century hooked rug in an auction catalog that we bought at our local flea market. Our rug design was adapted from the catalog rug. Karl hooked the rug with overdyed recycled *as is* wool. Size: 16" x 36 ½".

Sign of the Parrot Tavern

Although many taverns were named after birds, it is unusual to find a tavern named after a parrot. The image of the parrot was used by haberdashers, ironmongers, goldsmiths, and toy-men. A practice more common in England than America used a live parrot in its cage placed outside the front door of the tavern as its sign. Variations of the parrot theme included the Green Parrot, Parrot & Cage, Parrot & Star, and the Parrot & Pearl.

Mary Jo used the parrot image from a Pennsylvania German fraktur drawing by Henrich Otto found in *The Gift is Small, the Love is Great* by Frederick Weiser to design the rug. Karl hooked the rug in 2009. Recycled wool was used for all but the parrot, which was hooked in new wool. Size: 29"diameter.

Raven & Ring Tavern

The image of the raven served as a symbol for royalty and the nobility in Scotland for centuries. It is found on Scottish coats of arms, weaponry and decorative arts.

As tavern and shopkeepers sought ways to draw attention to their signs, one technique used crushed glass glued to the sign to reflect light. The raven has a reputation for being a curious bird attracted to shiny objects often found in its nest. The ring in our rug was hooked with synthetic fabric that had glimmering gold and silver fibers.

Mary Jo designed the rug and Karl hooked it in 2011. The circular shape of the ring was replicated in the background. Size: 29" x 45 ½".

Bird-in-Hand Tavern

Bird-in-Hand Taverns were common in Great Britain and early America. Several sources influenced the origin of this name. The proverb "A bird in hand is worth two in the bush" is a fitting reminder to both the customer and innkeeper that future promises do not compare to what is in hand. The medieval sport of hawking refers to a falconer holding a bird in his leather gloved hand.[31] A live bush hanging in front of a building also served as an ancient tavern sign.[32]

The Bird-in-Hand Tavern in Newtown, Pennsylvania housed Hessian officers captured at the Battle of Trenton on Christmas Day 1776.[34] It currently serves as a private residence.   The Bird in Hand Tavern in old Philadelphia had a sign with a sportsman holding a dead bird in one hand and on the other side of the sign were two birds in a bush, out of the sportsman's reach.[35]

One of our favorite stories is about a colonial tavernkeeper whose sign suggested that a drink at his Bird-in-Hand Tavern was the equivalent of two drinks from his competitor at The Bush.[33]

Our rug pattern was adapted from the Rose's Inn sign in the Connecticut Historical Society collection and the contemporary Bird-in Hand Tavern sign in Newtown, Pennsylvania. Designed by Mary Jo and hooked by Karl in 2008. Size: 27"x 32".

Masonic Themes

The compass and the square are Masonic emblems that appear on many signboards. These symbols were used as code to identify taverns that were congenial meeting places for members of the brotherhood of Freemasons. Well known Masons included founding fathers, George Washington, Sam Adams and John Hancock. Notable exceptions were Thomas Jefferson and John Adams. Whigs and Tories also gathered in taverns where the proprietors were sympathetic to their views.

Beemer's Inn

The Freemasons held their meetings in taverns and in some cases had an entire room dedicated to their exclusive use. Freemason emblems, compass, square and All Seeing Eye, appeared on tavern signs welcoming members.

The original sign for Beemer's Inn is in the Smithsonian Institution collection. It served as inspiration for this rug. Karl hooked the rug in 2009. Wool from six sport coats was used in the background. Overdyed white skirts were used in the background of the central image. Some new wool was also used. Size: 49"x28".

The Green Dragon Tavern

The dragon appearing on tavern and trade signs is one of the oldest British heraldic images. The Green Dragon was the most frequently used tavern name. [36] Dragon images were also used by apothecaries.

The Green Dragon Tavern in old Boston was the meeting place for the Sons of Liberty, the Boston Committee of Correspondence and the North End Caucus; all were active in the revolutionary movement. The Boston Tea Party was planned at the Green Dragon. The royal governor described the tavern as a "nest of sedition" and Daniel Webster called it the "Headquarters of the Revolution." In 1764, the building was purchased by the Masons of St. Andrew's Lodge. The tavern, located in the basement, continued to operate while the Masons used the upper floors. The building no longer exists, but a 1773 ink and watercolor drawing still survives. "Where we met to Plan the Consignment of a few Shiploads of Tea Dec 16 1773" appears on the bottom of the drawing with the Masonic compass and square found in the upper left corner. [37]

Mary Jo adapted the rug pattern from the surviving 1773 drawing in the American Antiquarian Society collection. Karl hooked the rug in 2009. White and cream colored skirts were overdyed with gold and yellow for the background. Size: 26" x 38".

Humorous Themes

Our colonial forefathers are often thought of as a serious lot, almost devoid of a sense of humor. Nothing could be further from the truth. Humor is frequently found in tavern names. To illustrate this, *The History of Signboards from the Earliest Times to the Present Day* by Jacob Larwood and John Hotten devoted a whole chapter to "humorous and comic" signs and another to "puns and rebuses." A rebus is a pictorial representation of words. A simple rebus for "I love you" would depict an image of a human eye, the shape of a Valentine heart and the letter U.

Silent Woman Tavern

The Quiet Woman, the Silent Woman and the Good Woman were popular names for taverns in the 18th and 19th centuries in England, Holland, Italy, and America. Each shared a common image of a headless woman. Today the name is perceived as humorous even though martyrs were pictured as headless or holding their heads in their hands. The Good Woman depicted a decapitated female saint. Anne Boleyn, Henry VIII's beheaded wife is also connected with the image.[38]

An account of a Philadelphia tavernkeeper who changed the name of his tavern from the Purple and Blue Tavern to the Quiet Woman created an uproar which led to the loss of patronage and sale of his tavern.[39]

While we were familiar with the name Silent Woman, we have not found an image of an old sign based on this theme. Therefore, Mary Jo designed the pattern without reference to a signboard Karl hooked the rug in 2005 with recycled wool. Size: 24" x 28".

Crofut's Inn

Crofut's Inn is an example of a rebus which consists of images and letters that represent words. Historically, a rebus was a visual device used to create a pun that alludes to a person's name. The crow and foot form the innkeeper's name, Crofut. The building represents the inn.

George Crofut operated his inn in Oxford, Connecticut from 1892 to 1910. "It is possible that Crofut's father may have used the signboard since he was operating a boarding house in Middlebury, Connecticut in 1880."[40]

Mary Jo adapted the pattern from the original sign included in the Connecticut Historical Society collection and featured in their book, *Lions & Eagles & Bulls*. Karl completed the rug in 2004. Size: 31 ½" x 33 ½".

Goat in Boots Inn

The Old Inns of England by A.E. Richardson is a rich source of names and information on old taverns. The original sign for the Goat and Boots tavern is attributed to the British painter, George Morland. The name, Goat in Boots, has its roots in England as do many early American tavern signboards. Records of a Goat Inn appear in Chelsea, England as early as 1663 and in Boston, Massachusetts in 1737. [41]

Mary Jo designed the rug using the image of an antique goat weathervane and added the boots. Karl hooked the rug in 2006. Red wool was used for the boots, wool from old blue skirts for the background and several brown herringbone sport coats for the body of the goat. An old green blanket was used for the ground. Size: 31 ½" x 27".

Hartwell Perry's Ordinary

Hartwell Perry's Ordinary, was a tavern located on Duke of Gloucester Street in Williamsburg, Virginia from 1782 to 1800. Since the original signboard is gone, we imagined it in the form of a rebus. "Hart" is an old word meaning stag or male deer. The hart, followed by the water well, creates the tavernkeeper's first name, Hartwell. "Perry" is an 18th century cider-like drink made from pears. Hence, the pear tree represents the tavern owner's last name, Perry. "Ordinary" is an old word meaning tavern. The building represents the ordinary.

The rug was designed by Mary Jo and hooked by Karl 2007. We used wool from a blue and white checked skirt for the sky, several green skirts for the fields and a navy blue blazer for the background behind the lettering. Karl hooked part of the rug during a visit to Colonial Williamsburg. The inspiration for the striped hart came from an antique appliquéd quilt. Size: 25" x 50".

Navy Yard Tavern

Puns and rhymes on tavern signs may have been used initially as memory devices to help patrons remember their favorite tavern. Punning became a popular sign of refinement as literacy improved. *Watson's Annals of Philadelphia* refers to "a sign on a tippling-house near the Navy Yard on which were paintings of a tree, a bird, a ship, and a mug of beer" with the following inscription:

"This is the bird that never flew, this is the tree that never grew, this is the ship that never sailed, and this is the mug that never failed."

Mary Jo created the pattern based on the verse in *Watson's Annals of Philadelphia*. Karl hooked the rug in 2009. An old blanket hooked well in a narrow cut for the lettering. Mary Jo's signature face peeks from behind the tree. Size: 38" x 44".

Dublin Inn

Irish immigrants began arriving in Bucks County, Pennsylvania in the early 1800s. By the time of the American Revolution, a tavern owned by two Irish brothers was in operation along the Newtown-Quakertown Road in Bucks County. According to local gossip, the brothers had a falling out and although they continued to run the tavern, each brother was on duty at a different time during the day. This resulted in the tavern patrons calling it the Double Inn with each brother serving his loyal customers.[42] Today the tavern renamed the Dublin Inn refers to the town where it is located.

The rug was designed by Karl and Mary Jo in 2011 and hooked by Karl using wool strips left over from previous projects. Found trim was added to the edge. Size: 25 ½" x 20".

Man Full of Trouble Tavern

The original sign was painted by the British painter William Hogarth for a London ale-house. Hogarth was known for his biting social commentary reflected in his engravings. The Man Full of Trouble reveals negative ideas about matrimony. The sign shows a man who stagers down the street carrying his gin drinking wife on his shoulders, a chain and lock around his neck with his wife and monkey pointing to "wedlock," a magpie on one shoulder pecking his head, a drunken sow in the corner, and a woman pawning her tea pot for more gin. Hogarth's engraving is inscribed "Drawn by Experience, Engraved by Sorrow" followed by the rhyme:

"A monkey, a magpie, and a wife, Is the true emblem of strife." [43]

An 18th century Philadelphia tavern operated by Martha Smallwood known as the Man Full of

Trouble Tavern also drew on the Hogarth engraving for its name. The building still stands in Philadelphia, but is no longer used as a tavern, although a contemporary tavern sign is posted on the site.

Mary Jo adapted the design from Hogarth's engraving. Karl hooked the rug. Size: 39 ½" x 49".

Dog and Pot Tavern

The Dog and Pot, Dog's Head in the Pot, Dog and Crock, and the Dog's Head in the Porridge Pot taverns were found in England, Boston and New York City. Ironmongers also used The Dog and Pot sign. Their wares included andirons, known as fire dogs, and iron pots.

In Holland, a person late for dinner is said to "find the dog in the pot" meaning that the empty pot has been given to the dog to lick out before being washed. Another interpretation is that the Dog's Head in the Porridge Pot refers to and mocks a sloppy housewife.[44]

Mary Jo designed the rug based on several images found in *Antiques & Arts Weekly*, a fraktur in *The Gift is Small, the Love is Great* and a three dimensional image of a London sign for the Dog and Pot. Karl hooked the rug in 2010. Size: 27 ½" x 4½".

Liberty, Commerce and Agriculture Tavern

Britain prohibited direct contact between colonial merchants and foreign ports before the American Revolution. Afterward, our seafaring merchants had sufficient vessels and resources to conduct far flung foreign trade. This Pennsylvania tavern sign is filled with symbols of the early republic. Liberty, commerce and agriculture are reflected in the eagle and shield, the anchor and globe, and the plough and wheat sheaf. The eagle and shield represent the victorious American nation, the globe and anchor reflect expanding commerce to all corners of the world including China, and the plough and wheat sheaf refer to the abundance of our fertile lands.[49] In the 1840s, when this sign was created, ninety per cent of Americans were farmers; their crops found ready markets at home and abroad.

Mary Jo adapted her design from an auction catalogue image. Karl hooked the rug in 2010. Brown herringbone sport coats were used *as is* for the body of the eagle. Overdyed white and buff skirts produced three shades of gold for the wheat. Mottled blue and white skirts provided wool for the globe. Size: 43"x48".

44

Phelps' Inn (Eagle Side)

A sign was generally hung from a post in front of the tavern. Most often the image was same on both sides of the sign; however, there are signs with different images on either side. The Phelps Inn sign is an example with a victorious, ferocious American eagle on one side and a docile lion representing the defeated British on the other side.

Captain Arah Phelps built the inn after serving in the American Revolution. The original Phelps Inn sign is in the Connecticut Historical Society collection. It was painted and signed by William Rice who was one of the few artisans to sign his work.[47] Karl adapted the pattern from the original sign and hooked it in 2011. Brown textured wool from several sport coats was used to hook the eagle's body. White and cream colored skirts and blazers were overdyed and used in the sky. The background was hooked horizontally allowing the central image to standout. Size: 38"x53"

Phelps' Inn (Lion Side)

The image of the Phelps' Inn lion is one of the most frequently copied folk art images and appears on the dust jacket of the Connecticut Historical Society's book, *Lions & Eagles & Bulls*. The sign was painted by William Rice who was an "ornamental painter" in Massachusetts and Connecticut in the early to mid-1800s and was one of the few sign painters who signed his name to his work. His advertisements noted that he "painted signs of all descriptions in the newest style as well as decorating carriages, coaches, fire-buckets, militia drums, furniture, fan-lights, and doors."[48]

Rice painted several signs with a somewhat docile, unthreatening lion that represented defeated Britain. Some of the signs had the lion chained to reinforce the message that England had been contained.

Mary Jo adapted the rug pattern from the original sign. The brown wool used for the body of the lion came from nine different tweed and herringbone sport coats. The painted sky in the original sign has worn away creating a weathered and mottled look. White wool skirts were overdyed to produce a similar effect. Several green skirts were used for the grass. Size: 40" x 56".

Eagle Themes

When the Declaration of Independence was adopted, a committee of three men – John Adams, Benjamin Franklin and Thomas Jefferson – was appointed to choose a symbolic image for the seal of the new nation. Their ideas were too complicated and several subsequent committees were appointed to find an acceptable image.[45] After the Revolutionary War, the symbol of the American bald eagle was proposed in 1782. The eagle embodied the spirit of the young republic and represented a free, independent people of the new nation. The image of the eagle with outstretched wings and legs continued to evolve until the final version was adopted by the Congress. [46]

The eagle is the most common image found on early American tavern signs. Tavernkeepers proudly and patriotically displayed the eagle on their signs. It was rarely shown in its natural state; instead the eagle was most often drawn in a stylistic form with a shield, holding arrows and olive branches in its talons.

R. Angell Inn

The American eagle grew in popularity as the symbol of our new nation. It appeared in myriad forms and shapes. The Connecticut Historical Society owns the Providence, Rhode Island sign for the R. Angell Inn and describes it, as follows:

> "The highly individualistic design of this sign has long been celebrated as a folk art masterwork. The central eagle is curiously heart-shaped, lending it an overstuffed quality, exacerbated by limp wings and scrawny feet. Covering its body are nine white and eight red bars – one stripe for each state in the Union in 1801." [50]

The anchor in the eagle's left foot echoes the anchor found on the seal of Rhode Island. Karl adapted and hooked the rug from the original in 2011. The shield was hooked with new wool. A blue stripe from a large piece of blue and green plaid was used with two dark green and blue herringbone sport coats for the background. Size: 40" x 24".

Patriotic Themes

Tavern signs with patriotic themes were very popular in the late 18th and early 19th centuries. Signs reflecting our English heritage were common prior to the American Revolution. The Kings Arms, The Three Crowns, and The Queen were names frequently used by tavernkeepers. Those names were no longer politically correct after the war ended successfully for the colonies. Many signs were repainted and replaced with names of war heroes such as George Washington, the Marquis de Lafayette and John Hancock. The American flag, the bald eagle and the rising sun appeared as patriotic images on tavern signs, china, silver, furniture, powder horns, and textiles.

Liberty Tree Tavern

Although the image for this tavern sign rug appears rather simple, it is a rebus with hidden meaning and would have been understood by our colonial forefathers. The yellow circle or sun at the top refers to the Sons of Liberty, a group of mostly artisans who were opposed to British rule. Their symbol was a pine tree known as the Liberty Tree.

The colonists used the image of the pine tree as a symbol of resistance to British authority. It appeared on coins legally minted in New England until the British revoked the privilege. The Liberty Tree tavern sign or Sign of the Pine Tree reflected the innkeeper's political views and was visual code welcoming those sympathetic to the reistance.[51]Travelers in the period of the American Revolution often walked or rode horses which meant that they needed to find care for their horses and for animals they might be taking to market. The term "entertainment" on tavern signs meant that food, drink and lodging were available. "For hors" meant that the same was available for horses.

Mary Jo adapted the pattern from the original Sign of the Pine Tree found in the Connecticut Historical Society book *Lions & Eagles & Bulls*. Karl hooked the rug in 2005 using *as is* recycled wool. A "hit or miss" pattern was used for the background. Size: 23 ½" x 48".

Buckman's Tavern

Buckman's Tavern is associated with the Concord and Lexington skirmish that began the American Revolution. At least thirteen historic taverns were located along the road from Lexington to Concord known as "Patriot's Path." Buckman's Tavern, one of the thirteen, was built around 1710 and was located across from Lexington's Common. Minutemen gathered there on April 19, 1775 to await the British after Paul Revere warned them "the British are coming." The wounded were cared for at Buckman's Tavern following the encounter. Today, the tavern is maintained as a museum.[52]

Jessie Turbayne's book, *Hooked Rug Treasury* includes a series of rugs hooked in the early twentieth century with images of historic New England buildings drawn in childlike fashion. The perspective is off, the letters are askew and windows are cock-eyed. The series inspired Karl to create a primitive Buckman's Tavern rug. It was relatively easy for him to draw a primitive building and letters on linen backing. Hooking was another matter. Rug hookers typically are trained to keep the lines of buildings straight and letters lined up evenly. It was counter-intuitive to hook them crookedly. The rug took much longer to hook because of all the irregularities in the design, especially in the background. Karl deliberately made the roof look like he ran out of the basic wool and had to use a different piece.

Karl designed and hooked the rug in 2009. Wool from old black, dark purple and dark gray sport coats was used *as is* for the background. Size: 27 ½" x 44 ½".

Bloody Brook Tavern

When the first settlers carved out what was to become the frontier town of Deerfield in northwestern Massachusetts in the 1660s the area was a dense wilderness with hostile Indians. Settlers lived in constant fear of Indian raids. Those fears became a reality in September 1675 when the colonists were completely outnumbered and nearly obliterated by Indian warriors on the banks of a nameless stream. Since that day, the stream has been known as the Bloody Brook.[53]

The original signboard no longer exists. Mary Jo designed the rug and Karl hooked it in 2012. He used new multi-colored striped wool for the building, multi-colored strips for tree trunks and leaves, and recycled red garments for the bloody brook. The sky and tomahawk were hooked with white blazers toned by soaking the wool in cold water with copper pennies and ammonia. The tomahawk was sculpted in the Waldoboro style, a raised form of hooking. Size: 36 ½" x 50".

Temperance Hotel

Drinking alcoholic beverages was an accepted part of daily life in the seventeenth and eighteenth centuries in America. Worker satisfaction and productivity depended heavily on daily liquor rations. Besides preparing men to feel "strong and able to work," alcohol was thought to promote relaxation. The Temperance Movement grew and influenced change in drinking habits during the mid-1800s. In the early stages, the goal was to replace distilled beverages with beer, cider and other fermented liquors.[54] The American Society for the Promotion of Temperance pressured tavernkeepers to restrict the sale of alcohol. Some towns refused to approve tavern licenses.[55] Many tavern owners discontinued the sale of all alcoholic beverages; others continued to sell ale, cider and wine, but not distilled alcoholic beverages such as whiskey and rum. Tavern signs reflected the temperance policy of the tavern owners. Signs for the Temperance House, Temperance Tavern and Temperance Hotel replaced existing signs.

The Temperance Hotel sign, circa 1826-1842, in the Connecticut Historical Society collection reflects the temperance sentiment and patriotic image of the American spread eagle. The rug is adapted from the sign and Karl hooked it in 2003. Size: 19" x 32".

Ringos Tavern

Philip Ringo was granted a license to operate a tavern in Hunterdon County, New Jersey in 1738. John Ringo assumed ownership of the tavern in 1766. Ringos Tavern was the meeting site for those in the county who resisted British rule in the years leading up to the Revolution. The local Sons of Liberty and Committee of Correspondence met at the tavern and the delegates to the Provincial Congress in Philadelphia were elected there. The Hunterdon County Militia was recruited and drilled at the tavern. Ringos Tavern continued to serve as a meeting site throughout the War. [56]

Mary Jo designed the rug and Karl hooked it in 2014 as part of Hunterdon County's 300th birthday celebration. The Liberty Cap was selected as the central image to reflect the tavern's association with the Sons of Liberty. The cap was hooked with blue wool which symbolized freedom. Size: 22" x 29".

Green Tree Tavern (Trenton)

This Trenton, New Jersey tavern was initially known as the Royal Oak. The name had changed to the Green Tree as noted in a September 20, 1779 diary entry by John Adams - "dined at the Sign of the Green Tree"- during his visit to Trenton.

Mary Jo designed the pattern based on a quote from the Marquis de Chastelleux, a major general in the French army and relative of Lafayette, who stayed at the Green Tree in 1780:

> "I found my headquarters well established in a good inn kept by Mr. Williams. The sign of this inn is a philosophical, or if you will, a political emblem. It represents a beaver at work, with his little teeth, to bring down a large tree, and underneath is written perseverance."[57]

"Perseverance" refers to the Americans prevailing over the British.

Mary Jo designed the rug based on the tavern name. Karl hooked the rug in 2014 as part of Hunterdon County's 300th birthday celebration. Size: 30"x42".

William Pitt Tavern

Tavernkeepers who were supporters of separation from England readily embraced the need to change their British themed tavern signs. Some loyalists resisted and needed coaxing. John Stavers' Earl of Halifax Tavern in Portsmouth, New Hampshire was named after a supporter of the King's policies and was a meeting place for loyalists. In 1777 a mob formed at the tavern and proceeded to cut down the posts supporting the Halifax Tavern sign. Stavers sent out his slave with ax in hand. He struck the mob leader, rendering him insane. Stavers was arrested and held for a few days. Shortly thereafter, Stavers changed the name of his tavern to the William Pitt, after the great British defender of colonial liberty. [58] Mary Jo created the pattern and Karl hooked it in 2015. Size: 29"x22".

Celestial Themes

Stars, moon, and sun appeared in antiquity as pagan symbols and eventually were adopted for Christian use. Over time the symbols migrated to tavern signs. They could be found in various colors and numbers. Combinations such as the Moon and Seven Stars, Sun and Horseshoe and Star and Garter were popular.

Sun Tavern

Taverns named after the sun were ubiquitous in the early history of the nation. As with other signboard images, The Sun came in variations and combinations including The Rising Sun, Setting Sun, Golden Sun, Sun & Anchor, and Sun and Horseshoe. [60]

The Sun Tavern in Bethlehem, Pennsylvania, was built in 1758 to accommodate visitors to the Moravian community. Patrons of the tavern included George Washington, Ethan Allen, the Marquis de Lafayette, John Paul Jones, and Alexander Hamilton. John Adams claimed it was "the best Inn I ever saw." [61]

There were several Sun Taverns in Boston during the 1700s including one owned by General Henry Dearborn; his sign had an image of a gilded sun with rays and the inscription: "The best Ale and Porter under the Sun."[62]

Mary Jo designed the rug based on examples of the sunburst found as decorative inlay on Federal era furniture. Karl hooked the rug in 2004. Size: 31 ½" x 33 ½".

Rising Sun Tavern

The Rising Sun had heraldic origins and it was believed that the name brought good luck to a new inn. [63] The good luck associated with the rising sun may have accounted for its use as a name for an American ship trading in the Caribbean and China in the late 1780s. [64] The sunburst became a popular early American symbol representing the ascendant, newly formed nation. The importance of the rising sun image significantly grew during the Constitutional Convention in 1787. The president of the Convention sat on a chair with a sunburst on the crest. Benjamin Franklin commented that during the ebb and flow of the debate he was unsure whether the sun was rising or setting. At the successful conclusion of the Convention, he said that the sun was surely rising.

In 2007, Foltz Pottery had an open studio day. Anyone attending could decorate a redware plate with designs based on Pennsylvania German folk art. We poured through resource books looking for potential design ideas. Karl wanted an image which could be used on a plate and a rug. We found a circa 1820 fraktur drawing of the Rising Sun Tavern in *The Gift is Small; the Love is Great* by Frederick Weiser.

Mary Jo adapted the tavern image for the rug adding a primitive bird and flower for balance. The name of the tavern was not added to the rug design consistent with the earliest tavern signs without text. Size: 17 ½"x28 ½".

Seven Stars Inn

The Sign of the Star originated in medieval times when a star symbolized the Virgin Mary. According to Helene Smith, author of *Tavern Signs of America*, "the seven stars symbol is thought to have stemmed from the Crusades of the Middle Ages; in England the title was believed to have referred to the seven sorrows of Saint Mary, or perhaps the seven virtues, or even the seven sins of man."[65] Freemasons consider seven to be the perfect number as reflected in their symbol of the seven pointed star. Others see a possible connection with the Big Dipper constellation. The star could be found on the signs of many London shopkeepers; cabinetmakers, chemists, druggists, embroiderers, goldsmiths, and silversmiths.[65]

Star Taverns were found in many cities in Pennsylvania, Massachusetts, New Jersey, Virginia, and South Carolina. The signs existed in various colors and combination; The Harp & Thirteen Stars, The Star and Three Mariners and The Moon and Seven Stars.[66]

Karl designed and hooked the rug in 2005. Size: 23"x 28".

Half Moon Inn

English literary history includes a reference to Ben Johnson who went to the Half Moon Tavern in London and found it closed. He went to the Sun Tavern and wrote this epigram: "Since the half moon is so unkind, to make me go about, The Sun my money now shall have, and the Moon shall go without."[67]

Like so many early tavern names, the Half Moon migrated from England to America in the 18th century. Variations include the Blue Moon, Half Moon & Seven Stars, Sun Moon & Seven Stars, and Dark-of-the-Moon.[68]

The Half Moon Inn is located in Newtown, Pennsylvania. Built in 1733, it is one of the oldest buildings in the community and currently houses its historical society. It inspired the rug which Karl designed and hooked in 2007. Size: 25 ¾" x 34".

Religious Themes

Religion played an important role in the lives of most early Americans. Religious symbolism found on old signboards was understood and appealed to those who passed by the signs for The Angel, Cross Keys, The Sign of the Bible, Heart and Bible, Lion and Lamb, The Red Cock, Adam and Eve's Garden, Noah's Ark, Rainbow and Dove, and Devil's Half Acre.

Three Nuns and Hare Tavern

Kirklees Priory lay within the grounds of Kirklees Park. A tavern probably stood on this site behind the priory during the 16th century. Following the dissolution of the monasteries in 1639 by Henry VIII, tradition indicates that three nuns from the priory may have taken over the tavern. [70]

Taverns named *The Three Nuns* were appearing in other towns as well. The addition of the *Hare* may be a playful attempt to draw attention to the tavern. Astrological and religious symbolism was also associated with the hare. Puritanism brought changes to the name; *Three Nuns* became *Three Widows* and *Three Sisters.*[71] The image of a nun in flowing habit may have influenced its use on the signboards of linen drapers and milliners as well.

Designed by Mary Jo and Karl and hooked by Karl in 2015. Size: 23"x29".

The Red Cock Tavern

The Sign of the Cock, one of the oldest tavern names, was in use at the time of the Romans. In Christian times it gained more prestige. Jesus said to Peter "I tell thee, Peter, the cock shall not crow this day, before thou shalt thrice deny that thou knowest me." At one point, a papal edict required that the image of the cock be installed at the top of every church as a symbol of Peter's betrayal. [73] Cock fighting was a popular "sport" in colonial America and often took place at the tavern. The Fighting Cock Tavern in New York displayed cocks fighting on its signboard. [74]

Karl designed and hooked the rug in 2008. The pattern was adapted from examples of old rooster weathervanes found in folk art books. Our goal was to hook a rug that looked like an old weathered signboard. Four to six brown textures were used for each background blocks. The letters were hooked with similar values to achieve the weathered look. Size: 24" x 25 ½".

The Gardenville Hotel

The Gardenville Hotel was rebuilt around 1871 on the site of the original 18th century Plough Tavern in Bucks County, Pennsylvania. It had interesting connections with the notorious Revolutionary War outlaws known as the Doan Family Gang.[76] The Doan boys were British sympathizers, horse thieves and robbers of local tax and fine collectors throughout the county. Rumor has it that the gang hid stolen money in the caves of the county. Treasure hunters continue to search the caves for treasure today.

Mary Jo photographed the inn and referenced it for her design. Karl hooked the rug in 2010. Brown tweed and herringbone sport coats were used to hook the stones in the building. Size: 24"x 23".

Blew Bell Tavern

The Sign of the Bell was popular with tavern owners and shopkeepers in England and America. The bell is found on signs in England as early as the 14th century.

The color blue represented freedom to the colonists. Many Bell Taverns were renamed Blue Bell during the American Revolution. In the 18th century spelling was not yet codified or consistent. Using "blew" instead of "blue" for the name of our sign is intended to illustrate that fact. Francis Symonds operated The Bell Tavern in Danvers, Massachusetts, which like Boston's Green Dragon, was a meeting place for The Sons of Liberty to "rabble rouse and condemn the English authorities." The tavern also served as a rendezvous for forces on the way to Lexington and later Bunker Hill.[81]

Mary Jo designed the rug and Karl hooked it in 2010. Signature faces peer out from behind the bell. Wool from a blue checked skirt was used for the inside of the bell; darker blue from several blazers for the top of the bell; new red wool for the background. Vintage fringe was added to the edge of the rug. Size: 29 ½" x 27 ¼".

The Cross Keys Hotel

The origins of crossed keys goes back to Biblical times and represents St. Peter who was given the "keys of heaven" (Matthew 16:18-19). During medieval times, monasteries displayed the crossed keys to symbolize safety for travelers who needed a place to rest and find food.[77] Large cities and smaller towns boasted Cross Keys taverns. According to one account "there were at least 50 taverns in the colonies called Cross Keys." [78] A tavern located in a county seat could be designated "within prison bounds" which meant the tavern was accessible to imprisoned debtors – a very profitable business. The Cross Keys in Burlington, NJ was such a tavern.[79]

Karl adapted the rug from the Cross Keys Hotel sign. The original sign is in the Bucks County Historical Society collection. During the War for Independence, British loyalists gathered at the Cross Keys. The tavern operated until 1906 when its license application was rejected. It opened again after Prohibition and operated until 1995.[80] The stone building still stands in the area known as Cross Keys.

Karl hooked the rug in 2010. Size: 30"x20".

General Tavern Signs

Blue Ball Inn

The Blue Ball Inn was built in 1769 in Shrewsbury Township, Pennsylvania and served as a stagecoach stop. A mechanical device hoisted or lowered a ball on a pole to signal the stagecoach driver. A ball hoisted to the top of the post directed the stage to "go right on." A lowered ball signaled that passengers were waiting at the inn.[54] Ball tavern signs wore many colors. A golden ball symbolized royalty and often identified Tory taverns, some used as meeting sites for British spies.[82] Variations on this theme include Red, Blue, Black, and Green Ball, and combinations, the Ball & Cap, Red Ball & Acorn, Plough & Ball, Bible & Ball, and Green Man & Ball. [83] A blue ball was used on the trade sign of Benjamin Franklin's father, a soap and candle maker.

Karl adapted the rug from a sign in the York County Heritage Trust collection and hooked it in 2005. Size 25" x 20".

Crooked House Tavern

The story of this rug refers to an old English mining town where years of mining operations left the land under the town honey-combed with tunnels. Town buildings eventually leaned as they sank into the ground. The Crooked House Tavern in South Staffordshire, England was built in 1765 as a farmhouse. It later served as a pub known as Siden House. "Siden" means crooked in the local dialect. Condemned as unsafe in the 1940s, the tavern was rescued by the installation of girders and buttresses.[85]

Karl designed the rug in 2008. Wool strips of red, burgundy, orange, and green were hooked in short interlocking curls and curves to form the tree tops. Green wool skirts, shirts and blazers were used for the field and a purple skirt was used for the house. Size: 31 ½" x 24 ½".

Loomis Inn

A decanter and wineglasses or a punchbowl depicted on a signboard reflect a tradition that signals the function of the buildings from which they hung.[83]The David Loomis' Inn sign is part of the Connecticut Historical Society collection. The 1811 date may have been added as an afterthought since it results in an unbalanced design.[87] The J. Kelsey Tavern sign in the Old Sturbridge Village collection has a similar image of a wine decanter and toddy glasses.

Mary Jo adapted the rug pattern from the sign. Karl hooked the rug in 2013. Wool from a checked skirt used to hook the decanter and glasses represents crackled paint on the old sign. Size: 18 ½ x 22 ½".

About Rug Hooking

We refer to what we do as "traditional" rug hooking to differentiate it from the contemporary craft of "latch-hook" rug making. Traditional rug hooking is indigenous to North America; there is no record of it coming with those who migrated here. It is unclear whether our form of rug hooking started in northern New England or the Canadian Maritime Providences.

By the second quarter of the 19th century, the rigors of daily life had sufficiently eased so that women started to have discretionary time to use for creative activities. The early rug hookers went to their rag bags for whatever scraps they could find to use for a decorative yet functional rug. An old piece of linen or burlap was used for the backing. A crude hook was made with a bent nail driven into a wooden handle. We can imagine a woman going to the fireplace for a piece of charcoal or coal to draw a primitive pattern on the backing. The simple images would be large and bold, perhaps a dog, horse or flowers from the garden. The rag bag fabrics were cut or ripped in strips and then pulled up with a hook to form loops. By the 1850s, printed rug patterns were available from peddlers and the local general store.

From those humble beginnings, interest in rug hooking has spread around the globe with international guilds sponsoring chapters in many cities. Local guilds and friends gather to hook in community centers, churches, libraries, and homes. Rug hooking instructors are available in many communities. Books, magazines, videos, and internet instruction are readily available as is hooking equipment, wool and other supplies.

Most rug hookers prefer to hook with 100% wool. It can be new wool bought off the bolt or recycled wool from used clothing found at thrift stores, rummage sales and flea markets. The wool can be used *as is* or overdyed creating wonderful possibilities. A number of rug hookers today are introducing other fabrics such as paisley, Sari ribbon and nylon into their mixed media work. Rug hooking like other art forms continues to evolve.

Hooking with Recycled Wool Clothing

Recycling garments for hooking rugs is an ideal way to provide an inexpensive source of wool. Thrift stores, flea markets and rummage sales can be productive sources of old woolen clothing.

<u>Wool or Blends?</u> -- Most rug hookers prefer to work with 100% wool. Some use an 80%-20 % blend if the fabric is special or a hard to find color. Most often the garment will have a label that shows the fabric content. If there is no label and you are unsure, there is an easy test you can use. Bleach dissolves wool, so put a piece of the fabric in a small container of fresh bleach. It will dissolve overnight (or sooner) if it is 100% wool. If it is 100% synthetic fiber, the bleach will do nothing to the fabric. If the fabric is a blend, the wool will dissolve leaving the synthetic residue. Another test that can be used is to take a small piece of fabric and burn it with a match. If it is wool, it will smolder and leave a soft ash. Synthetic fabric will leave a hard residue and give off the smell of burning plastic. With experience you can also tell by the sound of ripping the fabric. Wool rips with a soft sound while synthetic fabrics have a harsher sound, almost like ripping plastic. Moth holes are a sure sign that it is wool or has wool in it. Used clothing with moth holes decreases its value and can generally be purchased for a much reduced amount. Make sure to wash the garment immediately after bringing it into the house.

<u>There's Wool and There's Wool</u> —Wool varies in thickness. Avoid thin wool generally used in men's suits and trousers. The wool in overcoats is normally too thick, although it <u>may</u> be useable if you are hooking in a narrow cut (#3 or #4). A tight weave will hook better than a loose weave which often frays. With experience you will get the feel of which wools hook and look best. Remember there are no hard and fast rules here.

<u>What Garments are Best?</u> -- Skirts provide the most wool with minimum waste. Pleated skirts are the best, but it does take time to open up the pleats. You can find some wonderful plaid and textured fabrics in wool skirts! Pants also produce minimum waste. Blazers and sport coats can be the source of great tweeds and herringbones. Wool scarves are another good source and easy to process with virtually no waste. Wool blankets can be used if they are not too heavy.

<u>How to Process Your Woolen Finds</u> -- When buying used garments from thrift stores, flea markets or rummage sales, it is important to wash them before you do anything else with them. You have no idea where the garment has been or whether it may contain moth eggs. <u>Do not bring the garments into the house until you are ready to wash them.</u>

The first thing to do is wash the garments in the washing machine using warm water and regular laundry detergent. Washing removes dirt, dry cleaning chemicals and any insect eggs. The fiber may also tighten somewhat depending on the wool. If you wash the garment before taking it apart, it eliminates fraying at the cut edges and reduces the amount of lint in the dryer. After washing, put the garment in the clothes dryer (normal cycle) with a fabric softener sheet. Drying can produce a lot of lint depending on the fabric. It is best to check periodically to remove excess lint.

Some wool will felt in the washing and drying process and become too thick for hooking. We have not been able to figure out what causes the felting; it seems to happen more with scarves and women's blazers. Not all the garments being washed and dried at the same time will felt which leads us to think it has something to do with the nature of the wool fiber.

The next step is to disassemble the garment. In the process, you can salvage the buttons and skirt linings. The buttons can be used to replace missing ones and for other craft projects. Skirt linings can be used to dye and marbleize wool. It is not necessary to take the time to cut open the seams. For a skirt, cut off the waistband, remove the zipper, remove the lining, cut off the hem and open any pleats. The process is similar for trousers. It takes more time to dissemble a blazer or sport coat. First cut off the sleeves, remove the lining and cut off the buttons and cuff. Next cut the wool from the back of the jacket.

The front panels of women's blazers and men's sport coats have an interlining that helps the garment retain its shape. Interlining can be made of fabric, netting or a paper like product. Interlining may be difficult to remove. If the garment is old, the adhesive may be dried out which allows the interlining to be pulled off easily. Otherwise, it can be a chore to pull it off. Some people do not even bother and simply discard that part of the jacket. The lining may be easier to pull off while it is still damp. It appears that the moisture from washing softens the adhesive. We now use the wool even if we cannot remove the interlining. Our thinking is that the manufacturer would not use an adhesive that is harmful to the fabric. If the wool is thin, the interfacing actually makes it a bit thicker.

A disassembled garment will result in pieces of wool that are irregular in shape. It is critical to cut the wool strips on the straight grain. All you need to do is to take the irregular shaped piece, make a small cut (1" or so) at one end and rip the full length of the piece. That creates a straight edge.

Dyeing with Skirt Linings

The linings from recycled skirts contain dye which can be leached out and used to dye wool. It is a simple process:

- Normally the rule is to wash recycled clothing before hooking with the wool. If you plan to use the lining remove it before you wash the garment. That will avoid the risk of washing the dye out of the lining.

- Roll a piece of dry wool with the skirt lining forming a "jelly roll" and tie it with a strip of wool.

- Place the jelly roll(s) in 3-4 inches of cold water in the dye pot.

- Add a slug of laundry detergent (non-bleach)

- Bring the water to a slow simmer and let simmer for about 30 minutes. You will see the color leach out into the water.

- Add ½ cup of white vinegar (5% acidy)

- Simmer until the dye is absorbed by the wool (normally takes 5–20 minutes).

- Turn off the heat and allow the water to cool

- Rinse wool in warm water, spin dry and put in dryer

The wool will have an interesting mottled look. Sometimes the dyed wool will be a different color than the lining. In any event, using skirt linings is an inexpensive way to get beautiful dyed wool.

Bibliography

Bayles, W. Harrison. *Old Taverns of New York*, NY: Frank Allaben Genealogical Co., 1915.

Boyer, Charles S. *Old Inns and Taverns in West Jersey*. Camden, NJ: Camden County Historical Society, 1962.

Callow, Edward. *Old London Taverns*, New York, NY: Brentanos 1901

Corballis, Paul. *Pub Signs*, Luton, England: Lennard Publishing Ltd, 1988

Crawford, Mary Caroline, *Little Pilgrimages Among Old New England Inns,* Boston: L. C. Page & Co., 1907.

Delderfield, Eric R. *Introduction to Inn Signs.* New York, NY: ARCO Publishing Co.1969.

Drake, Samuel Adams. *Old Boston Taverns and Tavern Clubs.* W. A. Butterfield, Boston, MA, 1917

Duess, Marie. *Colonial Inns and Taverns of Bucks County.* Charlestown, SC: History Press, 2007.

Earle, Alice Morse. *Stage-Coach and Tavern Days.* New York: MacMillan, 1900.

Forbes, Allan. *Taverns and Stagecoaches of New England.* Boston, MA: The Rand Press, 1953.

Forbes, Allan. *Taverns and Stagecoaches of New England, Volume 11.* Boston, MA: The Rand Press, 1954.

Garvin, Donna-Belle & James L. Garvin. *On the Road North of Boston: New Hampshire Taverns and Turnpikes 1700-1900.* University Press of New England, 1988.

Heal, Ambrose. *The Sign Boards of Old London Shops.* London, England: Portman Books, 1957.

Larkin, Jack. *The New England County Tavern.* Sturbridge, MA: Old Sturbridge Village, 1943.

Larwood, Jacob. *The History of Signboards from the Earliest Times to the Present Day.* London, England: Chatto & Windus, 1908.

Lathrop, Elsie. *Early American Inns and Taverns.* New York, NY: Robert M. McBride Co., 1926.

Matz, B. W. *Dickensian Inns & Taverns.* New York, NY: Charles Scribner's Sons, 1922

Rice, Kym S. *Early American Taverns: for the Entertainment of Friends and Strangers.* Chicago, IL: Regnery Gateway, 1983.

Richardson, A. E. *The Old Inns of England.* London, England: Charles Scribner's Sons, 1935.

Rivinus, Willis M. *Early Taverns of Bucks County.* New Hope, PA: n. p. 1965.

Schoelwer, Susan P. *Lions & Eagles & Bulls: Early American & Inn Signs from the Connecticut Historical Society.* Princeton University Press, 2000.

Smith, Helene. *Tavern Signs of America - Catalog.* Greenburg, PA: McDonald/Sward Publishing Co., 1988.

Smith, Helene. *Tavern Signs of America - History.* Greensburg, PA: McDonald/Sward Publishing, Co., 1989.

Watson, John F. *Annals of Philadelphia and Pennsylvania in the Olden Time (Volume 3). Philadelphia*, PA.: Leary, Stuart Co., 1927.

Welsh, Peter C. *The Art of Enterprise: A Pennsylvania Tradition.* Lebanon, PA: Pennsylvania Historical and Museum Commission in concert with Landis Valley Associates, 1983.

Woerner, H. Ray. *The Taverns of Early Lancaster and the Later-Day Hotels.* (Vol. 73 No. 2 Journal of the Lancaster Historical Society). Lancaster, PA: Lancaster Historical Society, 1969.

Zingaro Clark, Kathleen. *Bucks County Inns and Taverns.* Charleston, SC: Arcadia Publishing, 2008.

Endnotes

1. Horace Mather Lippincott & Thornton Oakley, *Philadelphia* (Macrae Smith Co., 1926), 80.
2. Susan P. Schoelwer, Editor, *Lions & Eagles & Bulls: Early American Tavern and Inn Signs from the Connecticut Historical Society* (Princeton University Press, 2000), 38.
3. Kym Rice, *Early American Taverns: For the Entertainment of Friends and Strangers* Chicago: Regnery Gateway, 1983), 23.
4. Allan Forbes & Ralph M. Eastman, *Taverns and Stagecoaches of New England, Volume II* (Boston: The Rand Press, 1954), 85-86.
5. Rice, 34.
6. Ibid, 81.
7. Alice Morse Earle, *Stage-Coach and Tavern Days* (New York: The Macmillan Company, 1922), 13.
8. Jacob Larwood and John Camden Hotten, *The History of Signboards* (London: Chatto &Windus, 1908), 1.
9. Ibid, 3-4.
10. Ibid, 4.
11. Ibid, 18.
12. Edwin Tunis, *the Tavern at the Ferry* (New York: Thomas Y. Crowell Company, 1973), 18.
13. Elise Lathrop, *Early American Inns and Taverns* (New York: Robert M. McBride & Company, 1926), vii.
14. Helene Smith, *Tavern Signs of America* (Greensburg, PA: McDonald/Sward Publishing Company, 1989), 22.
15. Schoelwer, 49.
16. Rice, 36-38.
17. Alexander Bannerman, Editor, *Colonial Tavernkeepers Volume XII* (Privately printed for the Flagon and Trencher Society, 2011), 2-3.Bannerman, Volume XII, 4-5.
18. William Hosley Jr. and Gerald W.R. Ward, Editors, *the Great River: Art & Society of the Connecticut Valley 1635-1820* (Hartford, Connecticut: Wadsworth Athenaeum, 1985), 174.
19. Bannerman, XIII, 2-3.
20. Sotheby's, *Important Americana Auction in New York, January 18 & 19, 2008*, Lot 260.
21. Larwood and Hotten, 155.
22. Kathleen Zingaro Clark, *Bucks County Inns and Taverns* (Charlestown, SC: Arcadia Publishing, 2008), 71.
23. Willis M. Rivinus, *Early Taverns of Bucks County* (New Hope, PA. 1965), 53-55.
24. Smith, 42-43.
25. Rice, 31.
26. Larwood and Hotten, 226.
27. Smith, 85.
28. Ambrose Heal, *The Sign Boards of Old London Shops* (London: Portman Books, 1957), 33, 63, 78, 103 and 109.
29. Smith, 85.
30. Schoelwer, 31.

31. Eric R. Delderfield, *Introduction to Inn Signs* (New York: Arco Publishing Company, 1969), 52.
32. Larwood and Hotten, 4.
33. Zingaro Clark, 10.
34. Marie Murphy Duess, *Colonial Inns and Taverns of Bucks County* (Charleston: History Press, 2007), 73.
35. John F. Watson, *Annals of Philadelphia and Pennsylvania in the Olden Time* (Philadelphia: Leary Stuart Co., 1927), 361.
36. Larwood and Hotten, 111.
37. Russell Bourne, *Cradle of Violence* (Hoboken, NJ: John Wiley & Sons, 2006), 181-182.
38. Larwood and Hotten, 454.
39. Watson, Volume III 363.
40. Schoelwer, 21,171, 237.
41. Larwood and Hotten, 440-441.
42. Rivinus, 39.
43. Larwood and Hotten, 456.
44. Ibid, 443-444.
45. Smith, 19.
46. Alan Snyder, *Patriotic Eagle Inlays on Federal Furniture* (Waldoboro, Maine: Main Antiques Digest, June 2010), 26-30.
47. Schoelwer, 11.
48. Ibid, 44-48.
49. Carl L. Crossman, *the Decorative Arts of the China Trade* (Woodbridge, Suffolk, England: Antique Collectors' Club Ltd., 1991), 16.
50. Schoelwer, 132, 203-204.
51. Ibid. 190.
52. Forbes, 69.
53. Samuel Chamberlain and Henry N. Flint, *Historic Deerfield: Houses and Interiors* (New York: Hastings House, 1952), 6-7.
54. Donna-Belle Garvin and James L. Garvin, *On the Road North of Boston: New Hampshire Taverns and Turnpikes 1700-1900* (Hanover: University Press of New England, 1988), 153-157.
55. Schoelwer, 48.
56. Charles S. Boyer, *Old Inns and Taverns in West Jersey* (Camden: Camden Historical Society, 1962), 205.
57. Ibid, 183.
58. Garvin, 141.
59. Smith, 76.
60. Larwood and Hotten, 499.
61. Smith, 76.
62. Samuel Adams Drake, *Old Boston Taverns and Tavern Clubs* (Boston: W.A. Butterfield, 1917), 69.
63. Smith, 76.
64. Tim McGrath, *John Barry an American Hero in the Sage of Sail* (Yardley, PA: Westholme, 2010), 353.Smith, 77.
65. Heal, 41, 63, 90, and 181.
66. Smith, 77.

67. Larwood and Hotten, 500.

68. Smith, 78.

69. Tom Grinslade, *Powder Horns —Documents of History* (Texarkana, TX, Scurlock Publishing Company, 2007), 36.

70. Tripadvisor.co.uk.

71. Larwood and Hotten, 320-321.

72. Ibid, 205.

73. Charles and Margaret Layland, *Weathervanes and Country Signs* (Kutztown, PA Folklife, Summer 1985), 19.

74. Smith, 85.

75. Watson, Volume 361.

76. Zingaro-Clark, 56.

77. Smith, 92.

78. Tunis, 54.

79. Boyer, 53-54.

80. Zingaro-Clark, 51.

81. Nancy Carlisle, *Cherished Possessions – A New England Legacy* (Boston: Society for the Preservation of New England Antiques, 2003), 197-199.

82. Smith, 94.

83. Larwood and Hotten, 482-483.

84. Smith, 94.

85. Ibid, 94

86. Frederick W. Hackwood, *Inns, Ales and Drinking Customs of Old England* (New York: Sturgis and Walton, 1909), 50.

87. Schoelwer, 205.

88. Ibid, 205.

89. Larwood and Hotten, 216-217.

90. Rric.org/winningthevote/biographies/william-bloss

About the Authors

Karl and Mary Jo Gimber have taken their mutual interest in American history and the love of all things old and translated it into hooked rugs. Together they have created more than one hundred historic sign rugs, representing eighteenth and nineteenth century tavern, trade, and farm signs, gravestones, old weathervanes, and folk art with political messages, historical references, religious themes and humor. In 2012, the Gimber's rugs were featured at Rug Hooking Week at Sauder Village in Archbold, Ohio. Their rugs have been included in Early American Life Magazine, Rug Hooking Magazine, the Wool Street Journal, ATHA Magazine, Rags to Rugs-Hooked and Hand Sewn Rugs of Pennsylvania, Hooked Rugs Today, and Contemporary Hooked Rugs.

The End

MARCH 21, 2016
1st day of Spring
13th proof
26 corrections made for next proof

Proof

Made in the USA
Charleston, SC
18 March 2016